D1042046

WHAT'S THE CONNECTION ?

• Amazing Links •
Among Seemingly
Unrelated Things

JAKE OLIVER

METRO BOOKS
NEW YORK

A QUIRK PACKAGING BOOK

This 2008 edition published by Metro Books,
by arrangement with Quirk Packaging, Inc.

Cover design by Nancy Leonard
Interior design by Lynne Yeamans

Metro Books
122 Fifth Avenue
New York, NY 10011

ISBN-13: 978-1-4351-0636-9

Printed and bound in Singapore

10 9 8 7 6 5 4 3 2 1

INTRODUCTION

Are you a trivia buff? Would you call yourself a quick thinker?
Okay then—tell me quick, what's the connection between the
following four things: Valencia, Mandarin, Jaffa, Cara Cara.

If you answered "They're all kinds of oranges," well, then you're
ready to tackle *What's the Connection?* The rules are simple. Each
right-hand page features a list with four items—it's up to you to
figure out the connection among them. But be warned, finding the
links can be a lot trickier than you think. Can't figure out the connection? Don't worry, just turn the page for the answer and, voilà,
you are instantly that much smarter than your friends and family.

If you make the connection consistently without breaking a
sweat, you may be ready to test your brainpower with the Big
Connections sprinkled throughout the book. These mind benders
challenge you to name the connection that binds as many as ten
seemingly unrelated things. *What's the Connection?* is also the
proud home of Factamazoids. Not to be confused with skimpy,
run-of-the-mill factoids, Factamazoids are amazing, substantial
chunks of knowledge that accompany each list, adding a fascinating extra dimension to each connection.

From serial killers to Care Bears, from common food additives to
frequently banned books, *What's the Connection?* moves from
subject to subject at a delightfully dizzying clip. These perplex-
ing pairings should keep trivia experts on their toes and novices
eagerly turning the page to find the answers.

WHAT'S THE CONNECTION

West European Hedgehog

Western Diamondback Rattlesnake

Fat-Tailed Dwarf Lemur

Dormouse

(flip page for answer)

ANSWER

West European Hedgehog + Western Diamondback Rattlesnake + Fat-Tailed Dwarf Lemur + Dormouse

Hibernating Animals

Factamazoid: HUMAN HIBERNATION

While the phrase *human hibernation* conjures up images of Austin Powers or astronauts from an Arthur C. Clarke story, scientists believe a new technique could one day put humans into a reversible and prolonged "hibernation-like state." Using hydrogen sulfide, a chemical humans and other animals naturally produce in their bodies, scientists have successfully induced hibernation in mammals, putting mice into a state of suspended animation for up to six hours before bringing them "back to normal life." Further research into the phenomenon could lead to medical advances in cancer treatment, trauma care, organ transplantation, and yes, even interplanetary travel.

WHAT'S THE CONNECTION

Bashful Heart

+

Funshine

+

Do-Your-Best

+

Share

(flip page for answer)

ANSWER

Bashful Heart + Funshine + Do-Your-Best + Share

Care Bears

Factamazoid: CARE BEARS AROUND THE WORLD

In 1981, American Greetings hired artist Elena Kucharik to illustrate a series of greeting cards featuring a group of colorful, teddy-esque bears. The name Care Bears was adopted, and a cultural icon of the 1980s was born. In 1982, Parker Brothers launched a line of stuffed toys featuring the characters from the cards, and soon afterward, the Care Bears starred in their own television special, *The Land Without Feelings.* The first Bears were called Bedtime Bear, Birthday Bear, Cheer Bear, Friend Bear, Funshine Bear, Good Luck Bear, Grumpy Bear, Love-a-Lot Bear, Tenderheart Bear, and Wish Bear. In most French-speaking countries, the Care Bears are known as *Bisounours* or "kiss bears." However, citizens of Quebec prefer *Les Calinours*, or "hug bears," in order to avoid causing confusion between the cuddly do-gooders and the slang *bizoune*, which in the local vernacular translates as *penis*.

Aileen Wuornos

+

Ed Gein

+

H.H. Holmes

+

John Wayne Gacy, Jr.

(flip page for answer)

ANSWER

Aileen Wuornos + Ed Gein + H.H. Holmes + John Wayne Gacy, Jr.

Serial Killers

Factamazoid: EDWARD GEIN

American serial killer Ed Gein, also known as the Ghoul of Plainfield, Wisconsin, gained infamy in the 1950s by murdering and butchering at least two women and committing bizarre, necrophiliac acts on corpses stolen from local graves. In November 1957, the Plainfield police found a nightmarish collection of trophies that Gein had fashioned from human body parts. Gein confessed to killing Bernice Worden and Mary Hogan, but swore that the rest of the corpses on his farm had come from robbing local graves. Gein is widely believed to be the blueprint for the character Norman Bates in Robert Bloch's novel *Psycho*. Gein is also cited as the inspiration for Leatherface, the homicidal, human skin-wearing villain of Tobe Hooper's 1974 cult film *The Texas Chainsaw Massacre*, and for the Buffalo Bill character in Jonathan Demme's *Silence of the Lambs*.

WHAT'S THE ? CONNECTION

Master

+

Schlage

+

Yale

+

KwikSet

(flip page for answer)

ANSWER

Master + Schlage + Yale + KwikSet

Lock Manufacturers

Factamazoid: LOCKSPORT

Since the ancient Egyptians devised the first wooden locks more than 4,000 years ago, people have been trying to find ways around them. In recent years, the hobby/sport of competitive lock-picking has become an increasingly popular pastime. Indeed, lock-picking has become organized, with numerous groups of enthusiasts gathering online and off to hone their unusual skills. Locksport, as it is known, has adherents on every continent. In the Netherlands and Germany, lock-picking contests have been popular for years, and champion lock-pickers are national celebrities. The most famous competition is the Dutch Open, which is organized by TOOOL (The Open Organisation of Lock-Pickers). Locksport enthusiasts also study locks, sometimes finding significant flaws. Although many lock manufacturers aren't too thrilled with the sport, some savvy companies have started asking TOOOL and their peers to evaluate a lock before commencing mass production.

THE BIG ● CONNECTION

Constantinople
+
New Amsterdam
+
Petrograd
+
Edo
+
York
+
Saigon
+
Queenstown
+
Bombay
+
Kristiania
+
Batavia

(flip page for answer)

Constantinople + New Amsterdam + Petrograd + Edo + York + Saigon + Queenstown + Bombay + Kristiania + Batavia

Former Names of Cities

CONSTANTINOPLE: **Istanbul**
NEW AMSTERDAM: **New York City**
PETROGRAD: **St. Petersburg**
EDO: **Tokyo**
YORK: **Toronto**
SAIGON: **Ho Chi Minh City**
QUEENSTOWN: **Cobh (Ireland)**
BOMBAY: **Mumbai**
KRISTIANIA: **Oslo**
BATAVIA: **Jakarta**

WHAT'S THE CONNECTION

Pittsburgh Crawfords

Indianapolis ABCs

+

Dayton Marcos

+

Baltimore Elite Giants

(flip page for answer)

ANSWER

**Pittsburgh Crawfords ✦ Indianapolis ABCs ✦
Dayton Marcos ✦ Baltimore Elite Giants**

Negro League Baseball Teams

Factamazoid: INDIANAPOLIS CLOWNS

Also known as the Cincinnati Clowns, the Miami Giants, and the Ethiopian Clowns, the Indianapolis Clowns built a national following in the 1930s as one of baseball's most theatrical teams. Though the Clowns always played competitive baseball—claiming the pennant four times in the 1950s—it was the Clowns's Harlem Globetrotters-esque comedy routines that filled the seats. In 1953, the Clowns hired Toni Stone, the first woman to play professional baseball on a big-league team, but they are best known as the team where Hank Aaron started his career. In 1952, the 18-year-old Aaron joined the Clowns as their shortstop and led the league with a .467 average. Major league scouts soon took notice of the powerful hitter, and the Boston Braves bought out his contract for $10,000 midway through his first season.

CN

+

Sears

+

Pisa

+

John Hancock

(flip page for answer)

ANSWER

CN + Sears + Pisa + John Hancock

Towers

Factamazoid: BOSTON'S TERRIBLE TOWER

Less than a month after being completed in 1972, Boston's tallest building, the 60-story John Hancock Tower, developed a sudden and mysterious problem with its windows. The giant panes of glass began to pop out without warning and shatter on the street below. Amazingly, no one was injured. Concerned that a building that spontaneously hurled massive glass panels at pedestrians might be a poor symbol for their business, the John Hancock Mutual Life Insurance Company replaced all 10,334 windows with 400-pound (181 kg) sections of half-inch (1.3 cm) tempered glass. Then, just to be safe, the company hired two permanent guards with the sole responsibility of spotting cracked panes before they tumbled to the sidewalk.

Pygmy Sperm

+

Common Minke

+

Right

+

Strap-Toothed

(flip page for answer)

ANSWER

Pygmy Sperm + Common Minke + Right + Strap-Toothed

Whales

Factamazoid: WHALE NAMES

Not surprisingly, many whales were given their names by the whalers who hunted them. The Minke whale takes its name from an eighteenth-century Norwegian whaler, infamous for ignoring whale-hunting size restrictions. Other whalers soon jeeringly referred to all small whales as "Minke's whales." The name stuck and was later formally adopted for this specific species. The strap-toothed whale is named for the two large teeth that "strap" its bottom jaw to its upper jaw. Right whales got their name from whalers who considered them to be the "right" whales to kill because they are big, slow, and tend to live close to land—not to mention that unlike other whale species, right whales float after death. The sperm whale's massive head has a cushion-like growth containing a clear, oily liquid. Whalers thought the mysterious fluid was the whale's sperm and called it *spermaceti* (whale sperm).

WHAT'S THE CONNECTION

butylated hydroxytoluene

+

propylene glycol alginate

+

acesulfame-K

+

sulphur dioxide

(flip page for answer)

ANSWER

butylated hydroxytoluene + propylene glycol alginate + acesulfame-K + sulphur dioxide

Common Food Additives

More than 2,800 additives appear on our food labels. Here are common uses of the four listed above. For information about their safety, see www.cspinet.org.

BUTYLATED HYDROXYTOLUENE: Also known as BHT, this antioxidant is added to fats, oils, and baked goods and snacks that contain oil to prevent rancidity.

PROPYLENE GLYCOL ALGINATE: A derivative of kelp, this substance is used as a thickening agent and foam stabilizer in ice cream, yogurt, candy, and beer.

ACESULFAME-K: This artificial sweetener is 200 times sweeter than sugar. It is used in baked goods, chewing gum, gelatin desserts, and diet soda.

SULPHUR DIOXIDE: This sulfite is used to prevent discoloration in dried fruit and potatoes and to inhibit bacterial growth in wine.

Factamazoid Challenge: FOOD ADDITIVE WORD SEARCH

The following words are hidden horizontally, vertically, or diagonally, either forward or backward:

aspartame

azorubine

benzoic acid

borax

indigo carmine

maltodextrin

norbixin

pimaricin

polysorbate 20

polysorbate 40

polysorbate 60

polysorbate 80

potassium sorbate

red 2G

sodium benzoate

sulphur dioxide

thaumatin

```
P P P o 8 E T A B R O S Y L L O P 2 G D E R
O O 4 I N D I G O C A R M I N E 4 o 2 I A O
L L L o M I 4 E T A B R O S Y L O P D C X 4
Y Y o 6 G X P O S O D I U M B E N Z O A T E
S S 2 E o O O L U M I X O U T 8 B 8 T C H T
O O E T N I L U L A S S L A o o E E X I A A
R o T A O D Y 4 P O Y I B o 4 6 A T A O U B
B 8 A B R R G o 8 L L R E O N B T A T Z M R
A E B R B U G 2 O P O L Y I R 2 E B R N A O
T T R O I H 2 P D S P Y C O A A R R A E T S
E A O S X P o 4 M E X I S D S X X O P B I Y
4 B S Y I L Y U X D R Y o G P S N S S O N L
o R Y L N U I U M A D E R 2 A I Y Y A R X O
C O L O U S L A M E N I B U R O Z A A B D O
R S O P S O L I Z O R U B I T E T O O A E P
A Y P A P Y P O L Y S O R B A T 6 P L T R 2
M L T N I R T X E D O T L A M I o U O E 2 D
I O U U B E N Z O L G 2 D E E R L P P 8 G E
P P R E D 2 F O O L Y S O R B A T E 4 o o R
```

(flip page for answer)

23

```
P P P o 8 E T A B R O S Y L L O P 2 G D E R
O O 4 I N D I G O C A R M I N E 4 o 2 I A O
L L L o M I 4 E T A B R O S Y L O P D C X 4
Y Y o 6 G X P O S O D I U M B E N Z O A T E
S S 2 E o O O L U M I X O U T 8 B 8 T C H T
O O E T N I L U L A S S L A o o E E X I A A
R o T A O D Y 4 P O Y I B o 4 6 A T A O U B
B 8 A B R R C o 8 L L R E O N B T A T Z M R
A E B R B U C 2 O P O L Y I R 2 E B R N A O
T T R O I H 2 P D S P Y C O A A R R A E T S
E A O S X P o 4 M E X I S D S X X O P B I Y
4 B S Y I L Y U X D R Y o C P S N S S O N L
o R Y L N U I U M A D E R 2 A I Y Y A R X O
C O L O U S L A M E N I B U R O Z A A B D O
R S O P S O L I Z O R U B I T E T O O A E P
A Y P A P Y P O L Y S O R B A T 6 P L T R 2
M L T N I R T X E D O T L A M I o U O E 2 D
I O U U B E N Z O L C 2 D E E R L P P 8 C E
P P R E D 2 F O O L Y S O R B A T E 4 o o R
```

WHAT'S THE ? CONNECTION

Belka

+

Strelka

+

Pushinka

+

Laika

(flip page for answer)

ANSWER

Belka + Strelka + Pushinka + Laika

Soviet Space Dogs

Factamazoid: JFK'S SOVIET SPACE DOG

During the 1950s and 1960s, the USSR sent dogs on suborbital and orbital spaceflights to determine whether human spaceflight would be feasible. In 1959, Soviet space dogs Belka (Whitey) and Strelka (Little Arrow) became the first Earth-born creatures to return from orbit alive. In retirement, Strelka had six puppies with a male dog named Pushok. In 1961, at the height of the Cold War,

Nikita Khrushchev gave one of these pups, Pushinka (Fluffy), to President John F. Kennedy's daughter Caroline. After undergoing an intense security inspection to make sure that she was not a spy dog, Pushinka caught the eye of Kennedy's Welsh terrier Charlie. It is said that JFK jokingly referred to the four pups that resulted from their union as *pupniks*.

B-I

✛

Ramune

✛

Teem

✛

Fruktsoda

(flip page for answer)

ANSWER

B-1 + Ramune + Teem + Fruktsoda

=

Lemon-Lime
Soda Brands

In the 1920s, recognizing that Coca-Cola was the undisputed king of soft drinks, Charles Leiper Grigg set out to create a non-cola hit. After modest success with his orange soda, Howdy, Grigg introduced Bib-Label Lithiated Lemon-Lime Soda in 1929. The name didn't go over very well, and Grigg changed it to 7-Up Lithiated Lemon Soda, and then to just 7-Up in 1936. (The original 7-Up contained lithium, a lightweight metal found in natural springs now used in batteries and for treating mental illness.) With the Depression in full swing and more than 600 other lemon-lime sodas on the market, Grigg worked hard to promote 7-Up, and by the end of the 1930s, 7-Up was one of the nation's most popular sodas.

WHAT'S THE CONNECTION

Testa

+

Hilum

+

Cotyledon

+

Radicle

(flip page for answer)

ANSWER

Testa + Hilum + Cotyledon + Radicle

Parts of a Seed

Factamazoid: GLOBAL SEED VAULT

In 2007, the Norwegian government completed the construction of a vast "doomsday vault" inside a mountain on an Arctic island to hold a seed bank of all of Earth's known crops. Conceived of as the ultimate safety net for the world's seed collections, the hollowed-out seed lair on the ice-bound island of Spitsbergen was designed to withstand nuclear war or any natural global catastrophes that would jeopardize the planet's food sources. The first shipment of seeds represented 268,000 distinct samples of seeds originating from different farms or fields around the world. Eventually the Svalbard Global Seed Vault will hold 4.5 million samples of seeds, encompassing almost every variety of the world's most important food crops. Permafrost will keep the vault temperature below freezing, and the seeds will also be protected by 3-foot (1-m) thick walls of reinforced concrete and high-tech explosive-proof doors.

WHAT'S THE ? CONNECTION

California, 1849

Australia, 1851

Klondike, 1897

Georgia, 1829

(flip page for answer)

ANSWER

California, 1849 + Australia, 1851 + Klondike, 1897 + Georgia, 1829

Gold Rushes and Years

Factamazoid: "WINDWAGON" THOMAS

After the 1849 California gold rush, inventors devised some strange ways to cross the plains quickly. In 1853, William Thomas proposed a "wind-powered prairie schooner," or "windwagon," which was 25 feet (7.6 m) long with four 12-foot (3.6-m) wheels. The power source, a single sail, would be attached to a 7-foot (2.1-m) mast. Thomas believed that a fleet of these vessels would revolutionize the freight-shipping industry. When he brought a prototype wagon to Fort Leavenworth for a demonstration to the U.S. Army, the wagon barreled across the plains at the advertised 15 miles per hour (24 kph), but soon spun out of control and crashed. "Windwagon" Thomas—the would-be CEO of the Overland Navigation Company—kept trying to perfect his invention but never managed to secure his windfall.

Neon

+

Krypton

+

Argon

+

Radon

(flip page for answer)

ANSWER

Neon + Krypton + Argon + Radon

Noble Gases

When electricity passes through the inert gas neon, the gas's electrons are knocked from their orbits, causing energy to be released in the form of a bright red light. In 1910, French inventor Georges Claude put the world's first neon lamp on display in Paris. People were amazed at the first neon signs, which were brightly visible even in daylight, and called them "liquid fire." Claude's associate sold the first commercial sign in 1912 to a Parisian barber. Then in 1913, a sign 3½ feet (1 m) tall was installed on the Champs-Elysees—it said "CINZANO" and was advertising the popular Italian vermouth. Neon signs came to North America in 1923, when Claude manufactured two lights to be used as signage for a car dealership in Los Angeles. The signs said "Packard" and were purchased by the dealership's owner, Earl Anthony, for $12,000 per sign.

THE BIG ● CONNECTION

SANAE IV
➕
Mario Zucchelli
➕
Georg von Neumayer
➕
Dome Fuji
➕
Amundsen-Scott
➕
Esperanza
➕
Macquarie
➕
Rothera
➕
Dumont D'Urville
➕
Mirny

(flip page for answer)

SANAE IV + Mario Zucchelli + Georg von Neumayer + Dome Fuji + Amundsen-Scott + Esperanza + Macquarie + Rothera + Dumont D'Urville + Mirny

Antarctic Research Stations

SANAE IV: **South Africa**
MARIO ZUCCHELLI: **Italy**
GEORG VON NEUMAYER: **Germany**
DOME FUJI: **Japan**
AMUNDSEN-SCOTT: **USA**
ESPERANZA: **Argentina**
MACQUARIE: **Australia**
ROTHERA: **United Kingdom**
DUMONT D'URVILLE: **France**
MIRNY: **Russia**

WHAT'S THE ? CONNECTION

Wrass

+

Clownfish

+

Planaria

+

Banana Slug

(flip page for answer)

ANSWER

Wrass + Clownfish + Planaria + Banana Slug

Hermaphroditic Animals

(animals capable of producing both eggs and sperm)

Factamazoid: HERMAPHRODITES

In biology, the term *hermaphrodite* is used to describe an organism that possesses both male and female reproductive organs. Simultaneous hermaphrodites, such as snails, slugs, and earthworms, have both male and female sexual organs at the same time. Mating earthworms act as either male or female when they mate, but commonly switch gender roles depending on the partner. Sequential hermaphrodites, such as clownfish, start life as one sex but change according to the needs of their group. Clownfish generally live in harems made up of a reproductive male and female and several nonreproductive males. If the female dies or is removed from the harem, the reproductive male will change its sex, replacing the female. The male's spot will be filled by one of the formerly nonreproductive males.

WHAT'S THE CONNECTION

Colcannon

+

Vichyssoise

+

Bubble and Squeak

+

Baeckeoffe

(flip page for answer)

ANSWER

Colcannon + Vichyssoise + Bubble and Squeak + Baeckoeffe

Potato Dishes

Factamazoid: POTATO WAR

In 1778, Bavarian elector Charles Theodore attempted to cede Lower Bavaria to Austria through a secret treaty. This didn't sit well with Frederick II, King of Prussia, and before you knew it, the War of Bavarian Succession was in full swing. Neither the Austrians nor the Prussians were able to gain a swift victory, and all told, there was very little actual fighting. Instead, each force focused on a prolonged and complex series of maneuvers to obtain food supplies or deny them from the enemy. This mostly added up to looking for potatoes or destroying potatoes, and the soldiers soon christened the conflict *Kartoffelkrieg*, or the Potato War. In 1779, when the potatoes ran out, Austria renounced its claims to Lower Bavaria, and the two sides signed a treaty, making the conflict Frederick the Great's last war.

WHAT'S THE CONNECTION

Red Wattle

+

Mulefoot

+

Pietrain

+

Vietnamese Potbelly

(flip page for answer)

ANSWER

Red Wattle + Mulefoot + Pietrain + Vietnamese Potbelly

Pig Breeds

Factamazoid: **BACON**

ONE SLICE OF BACON OFFERS THE FOLLOWING:

139 calories

10 g total fat (3 g saturated,
1 g polyunsaturated,
5 g monounsaturated)

29 mg cholesterol

631 mg sodium

0 g carbohydrates

10 g protein

0% of the daily recommended
value of Vitamin A, Vitamin C,
Calcium, but 15% niacin and
phosphorous

WHAT'S THE ? CONNECTION

I Know Why the Caged Bird Sings

The Chocolate War

The Adventures of Huckleberry Finn

Of Mice and Men

(flip page for answer)

ANSWER

I Know Why the Caged Bird Sings + *The Chocolate War* +
The Adventures of Huckleberry Finn + *Of Mice and Men*

Frequently Banned Books

Factamazoid: TWAIN VS. ALCOTT

Originally published in 1884, Mark Twain's *The Adventures of Huckleberry Finn* was controversial from the start. In 1885, *Little Women* author Louisa May Alcott and a committee of concerned citizens succeeded in banning the book from the Public Library of Concord, Massachusetts. In her condemnation of the novel, Alcott declared: "If Mr. Clemens cannot think of something better to tell our pure-minded lads and lasses, he had best stop writing for them." In a letter to his publisher, Charles Webster, Twain retorted: "The Committee of the Public Library of Concord, Mass., have given us a rattling tip-top puff which will go into every paper in the country. They have expelled Huck from their library as 'trash and suitable only for the slums.' That will sell 25,000 copies for us sure."

WHAT'S THE CONNECTION

Yocco's

➕

Pink's

➕

Nathan's

➕

Swanky Frank's

(flip page for answer)

ANSWER

Yocco's + Pink's + Nathan's + Swanky Frank's

Famous Hot Dog Stands

Factamazoid: COMPETITIVE EATING

In the wake of recent televised coverage of the Nathan's Famous Fourth of July International Hot Dog-Eating Contest, held each July 4 on Coney Island, the popularity of competitive eating has bloated. Some notable competitive-eating records include:

SPAM: Richard LeFevre
6 pounds (2.7 kg) of SPAM from the can: 12 minutes

EGGS: Sonya Thomas
65 hard-boiled eggs:
6 minutes, 40 seconds

COW BRAINS: Takeru Kobayashi
57 brains (17.7 lbs, 8 kg total):
15 minutes

MAYONNAISE: Oleg Zhornitskiy
4 32-ounce (.9 kg) bowls of mayonnaise: 8 minutes

BUTTER: Don Lerman
7 quarter-pound (.11 kg) sticks of salted butter: 5 minutes

AND THERE'S ALWAYS ROOM FOR . . . GELATIN DESSERT: Steve Lakind 7 16-ounce (.45 kg) portions: 3 minutes

Anglerfish

+

Brolga Cranes

+

Wolves

+

Termites

(flip page for answer)

ANSWER

Anglerfish + Brolga Cranes + Wolves + Termites

Animals That Mate for Life

Factamazoid: ANGLERFISH

While it is technically true that anglerfish mate for life, the partnership is hardly romantic. As a male anglerfish matures, his digestive system degenerates, making him incapable of feeding independently. Using large nostrils, the male follows the scent given off by a female angler. The parasitic male bites through the skin of the female and attaches himself to his mate. The circulatory systems of the two fish fuse, and from that point on the male is completely dependent on the female. Gradually, the male angler's body begins to degenerate. He loses his eyes, tail, fins—pretty much everything—until he is nothing more than a small blob of testes. As the female releases eggs, hormones in her blood trigger fertilization. This extreme difference between the sexes ensures that, when the female is ready to spawn, she never has to look far for a mate.

WHAT'S THE ? CONNECTION

Irukandji

+

Lion's Mane

+

Sea Nettle

+

Habu Kurage

(flip page for answer)

ANSWER

Irukandji + Lion's Mane + Sea Nettle + Habu Kurage

Poisonous Jellyfish

Factamazoid: SESAME JELLYFISH RECIPE

$^1/_2$ lb (1 kg) prepared shredded edible jellyfish (*Rhopilema esculenta*), rinsed well and drained

2 tsp (10 ml) light soy sauce

3 tbsp (45 ml) sesame oil

2 tsp (10 ml) white rice vinegar

2 tsp (10 ml) sugar

3 tbsp (45 ml) white sesame seeds, toasted

1. Bring a large pot of water to a boil and pour the hot water over the jellyfish. Let the jellyfish sit in the water for about 15 minutes or until tender. Plunge the jellyfish in a large bowl of cold water and drain. Repeat the process with boiling water and cold water at least 6 times. Pat the jellyfish dry between paper towels and set aside.

2. Mix soy sauce, sesame oil, vinegar, and sugar in a small bowl. Toss the jellyfish well in this sauce and let it sit for at least 30 minutes. Garnish with the sesame seeds. Serves four as part of a complete meal or two as a single dish.

WHAT'S THE CONNECTION

Toto

➕

American Standard

➕

Eljer

➕

Kohler

(flip page for answer)

ANSWER

Toto + **American Standard** + **Eljer** + **Kohler**

Toilet Manufacturers

Factamazoid: TOILET-FLUSH MYTH

According to a longstanding story, toilets in the northern hemisphere flush clockwise while those in the southern hemisphere flush counterclockwise. A fascinating tidbit of infotainment, but alas, it isn't true. The misconception is based on the assumption that the Coriolis effect, resulting from the Earth's rotation, will make water behave differently in different locations. This concept is not entirely off the mark—the twisting effect of the Coriolis force is real and does influence large forces like the movement of air masses, as in tropical storms and hurricanes. The problem is that this effect is too subtle and slow to influence quick or small events, such as the flushing of a toilet. Toilets and sinks drain in the directions they do because of the way water is directed into them.

WHAT'S THE CONNECTION

Agni

➕

Indra

➕

Ganesha

➕

Surya

(flip page for answer)

WHAT'S THE CONNECTION

ANSWER

Agni + Indra + Ganesha + Surya

Hindu Gods

Factamazoid: GANESHA'S BIRTH

In Hinduism, the elephant-headed Ganesha is one of the most popular and venerated Gods. He is known as the Lord of Good Fortune and also the Destroyer of Obstacles. There are several accounts of his birth, but the most popular version claims that Ganesha was created by the goddess Parvati because her husband Shiva (Lord of Destruction) refused to respect her privacy. One day Parvati sculpted a young boy from sandalwood paste and told him to guard her door while she bathed. Later, when the young boy would not let Shiva enter, Shiva cut off the boy's head. Parvati, in her rage and grief, vowed to destroy the heavens and the earth. To pacify his wife, Shiva had his followers bring the head of the first living being they encountered, which happened to be an elephant. The elephant's head was placed on the boy's body, and he was brought back to life.

WHAT'S THE CONNECTION

Ludwig van Beethoven

Gabriel Fauré

Bedrich Smetana

William Boyce

(flip page for answer)

ANSWER

Ludwig van Beethoven + Gabriel Fauré + Bedrich Smetana + William Boyce

Deaf Composers

Factamazoid: BEETHOVEN'S DEATH—MYSTERY SOLVED

More than 150 years after Ludwig van Beethoven's death, scientists have concluded that the great composer was a victim of lead poisoning. When Beethoven died, a musician named Hiller clipped a lock of his hair. Via a circuitous path, eventually the 582 strands of hair were auctioned by Sotheby's, selling for $7,300 to the Brilliant Center for Beethoven Studies. The Argonne National Laboratory discovered a lead concentration of more than 100 times the normal level. It is speculated that Beethoven unwittingly poisoned himself during treatments at mineral spas. Lead poisoning causes nerve damage (which could explain his deafness), brain damage (which might explain his manic depression), and horrible intestinal cramps (which would explain his persistent abdominal pain and death).

THE BIG ● CONNECTION

Georges Prosper Remi

⊕

Charles-Edouard Jeanneret-Gris

⊕

Mary Anne Evans

⊕

Emmanuel Radnitzky

⊕

Domenicos Theotokopoulos

⊕

Theodore Geisel

⊕

Josip Broz

⊕

Aurore Dupin

⊕

Samuel Clemens

⊕

Edison Arantes do Nascimento

(flip page for answer)

ANSWER

Georges Prosper Remi + Charles-Edouard Jeanneret-Gris + Mary Anne Evans + Emmanuel Radnitzky + Domenicos Theotokopoulos + Theodore Geisel + Josip Broz + Aurore Dupin + Samuel Clemens + Edison Arantes do Nascimento

Birth Names of People with Famous Pseudonyms

GEORGES PROSPER REMI: **HERGÉ**

CHARLES-EDOUARD JEANNERET-GRIS: **LE CORBUSIER**

MARY ANNE EVANS: **GEORGE ELIOT**

EMMANUEL RADNITZKY: **MAN RAY**

DOMENICOS THEOTOKOPOULOS: **EL GRECO**

THEODORE GEISEL: **DR. SEUSS**

JOSIP BROZ: **TITO**

AURORE DUPIN: **GEORGE SAND**

SAMUEL CLEMENS: **MARK TWAIN**

EDISON ARANTES DO NASCIMENTO: **PELÉ**

WHAT'S THE CONNECTION

Senesino

+

Porporino

+

Farinelli

+

Nicolini

(flip page for answer)

ANSWER

Senesino + Porporino + Farinelli + Nicolini

Famous Castrati

Factamazoid: THE CASTRATO

In the sixteenth through the eighteenth centuries, women were forbidden on the stage, making male sopranos in opera common-place. In order to prevent their voices from changing at puberty, the finest boy sopranos were picked by music masters for castration. Though this practice seems shocking by contemporary standards, castrati were the rock stars of their time, possessing the high voice of a boy soprano but the lung power of a baritone or tenor. At the height of their popularity in Italy, about 4,000 boys were castrated each year. The last premiere of an opera featuring a castrato was in 1824, and the last performance of a castrato in London was in 1844. By 1870, the Italian government had banned castration. The last performing castrato, Alessandro Moreschi, was reportedly applauded by crowds with the cheer "*Eviva il coltello*" ("Long live the knife!").

Rebecca Nurse

➕

Sarah Good

➕

John Proctor

➕

Giles Corey

(flip page for answer)

ANSWER

Rebecca Nurse + Sarah Good + John Proctor + Giles Corey

People Executed for Witchcraft in Salem, Mass., 1692

Factamazoid: WITCHCRAFT AND THE CODE OF HAMMURABI

The appropriate method of detecting and punishing witchcraft has been a central concern of legal codes since ancient times. Written in the eighteenth century B.C., the Babylonian Code of Hammurabi addressed witchcraft in the following manner: If a man cast a spell on another man "without justification," the man upon whom the spell was placed had to "plunge into the holy river." If he drowned, the man who cast the spell got his house. If he lived, the man who cast the spell was killed, and his victim got his house. It is interesting to note that the laws concerning witchcraft are the first laws listed in the Code, reflecting ancient Babylonians' strong belief in the existence of supernatural forces.

Clove

+

Buntline

+

Rolling Magnus

+

Cow

(flip page for answer)

ANSWER

Clove + Buntline + Rolling Magnus + Cow

Knots

Factamazoid: KNOT MAGIC

From ancient times, the tying of knots has been closely linked with the practice of magic and witchcraft. The Egyptian goddess Isis's sacred symbol, the tat, was known as the Knot of Fate, and her priestesses were said to control the wind by tying their hair or blowing on knots. Similarly, the Greek goddess Circe was said to control the powers of creation and destruction by knotting and braiding her hair, and the Norns, the Norse Triple Fate goddesses, were said to possess similar powers. For centuries, certain women from Finland, Lapland, and Scotland were known for making magic knots to control wind and rain. Sailors often went to these sea witches for their "wind-knots" and commonly carried them on board ships in case they had to call up a wind. British witches were thought to be able to control a nosebleed by tying knots in a red thread.

WHAT'S THE ? CONNECTION

Belgrano

+

Mary Rose

+

Bismarck

+

Lusitania

(flip page for answer)

ANSWER

Belgrano + *Mary Rose* + *Bismarck* + *Lusitania*

Famous Sunken Ships

Factamazoid: SVALBARD SHIPWRECK SURVIVORS

In 1743, a Russian whaling ship was blown off course in the Arctic and trapped in ice off the coast of Svalbard (Spitzbergen). Four of the crew went ashore with only two days' worth of supplies in search of an abandoned hut they believed was on the island. To their delight, they found the hut, and they trekked back to tell their shipmates the good news. Unfortunately, when they returned the ship and crew had vanished, having apparently been crushed by the ice and sunk. With only the minimal provisions from their scouting mission, the crew endured more than six years of endless winter. Using a bow and arrows made from driftwood—Svalbard has no trees—they shot nine attacking polar bears. They survived largely on reindeer meat, killing 250 of the animals during their ordeal. Finally, they were rescued by another ship blown off course and returned home.

WHAT'S THE CONNECTION

Francisco Scaramanga

+

Ernst Blofeld

+

Hugo Drax

+

Le Chiffre

(flip page for answer)

ANSWER

Francisco Scaramanga + **Ernst Blofeld** +
Hugo Drax + **Le Chiffre**

Bond Villains

Factamazoid: FROM JFK WITH LOVE

In 1962, *Dr. No* enjoyed worldwide success as the first film adaptation of Ian Fleming's popular James Bond novels. When deciding which novel to adapt next, producers Albert R. Broccoli and Harry Saltzman got an unexpected nudge from President John F. Kennedy, when *Life* magazine listed Fleming's novel *From Russia with Love* as one of his ten favorite books. In his 1964 book *Death of a President*, William Raymond Manchester notes that *From Russia with Love* was the last motion picture JFK ever saw, on November 20, 1963, in the White House—days before his assassination. Though the film made its world premiere at the Odeon Leicester Square in London on October 10, 1963, its US release was delayed until May 27, 1964, due to the political climate after Kennedy's assassination.

WHAT'S THE CONNECTION

Encke

➕

Halley

➕

Hale-Bopp

➕

Kirch

(flip page for answer)

ANSWER

Encke + Halley + Hale-Bopp + Kirch

Comets

Factamazoid: HEAVEN'S GATE

Over the centuries, civilizations around the world have seen comets as divine omens. In 1997, Major Applewhite, leader of the American Heaven's Gate religious group, convinced 38 followers to kill themselves so that their souls could take a ride on a spaceship that they believed was carrying Jesus behind the comet Hale-Bopp. The members consumed phenobarbital mixed with vodka—or in some cases pudding or apple-sauce—before securing plastic bags around their heads to induce asphyxiation. They were found lying peacefully in their bunk beds, their faces and chests covered by a square of purple cloth. Each member carried a five dollar bill and three quarters. All 39 were dressed in identical black shirts and sweat pants, brand-new black-and-white Nike tennis shoes, and armband patches reading, "Heaven's Gate Away Team."

THE BIG ! CONNECTION

221B Baker Street

99 rue de Rivoli

10 Downing Street

Bennelong Point

1060 West Addison Street

263 Prinsengracht

1600 Pennsylvania Avenue

350 Fifth Avenue

(flip page for answer)

ANSWER

221B Baker Street + 99 rue de Rivoli + 10 Downing Street + Bennelong Point + 1060 West Addison Street + 263 Prinsengracht + 1600 Pennsylvania Avenue + 350 Fifth Avenue

Famous Addresses

221B BAKER STREET: **Sherlock Holmes residence, London, England**

99 RUE DE RIVOLI: **Musée du Louvre, Paris, France**

10 DOWNING STREET: **British Prime Minister's residence, London, England**

BENNELONG POINT: **Sydney Opera House, Sydney, Australia**

1060 WEST ADDISON STREET: **Wrigley Field, Chicago, USA**

263 PRINSENGRACHT: **Anne Frank's family residence during Nazi Occupation, Amsterdam, Holland**

1600 PENNSYLVANIA AVENUE: **The White House, Washington, D.C., USA**

350 FIFTH AVENUE: **Empire State Building, New York City, USA**

WHAT'S THE ? CONNECTION

Zuppa di Pesce

Cotriade

Fugu-Chiri

Cioppino

(flip page for answer)

73

ANSWER

Zuppa di Pesce + Cotriade + Fugu-Chiri + Cioppino

Fish Soups

Factamazoid: FUGU

Fugu, better known as puffer or blowfish, is one of the most revered dishes in Japanese cuisine. It can also be 1,250 times more poisonous than cyanide. Fugu chefs are required to pass a strict written exam and are tested by preparing and eating fugu. Despite the care taken in preparation, as many as 200 people are poisoned each year, with up to half of the victims dying. Victims experience acute paralysis, respiratory distress, convulsions, cardiac arrhythmia, and speech impairment. Death usually occurs within hours, but some patients exist in a zombielike state for days before recovering. Despite these dangers—or perhaps, because of them—fugu remains the food of choice for the adventurous. According to Japanese tradition, the emperor is the only person forbidden to eat fugu—the rest of the country is free to take their chances.

WHAT'S THE ? CONNECTION

Hypothalamus

➕

Testes

➕

Pituitary

➕

Adipose Tissue

(flip page for answer)

ANSWER

Hypothalamus + Testes + Pituitary + Adipose Tissue

Glands of the Endocrine System

Rankine

+

Celsius

+

Kelvin

+

Fahrenheit

(flip page for answer)

ANSWER

Rankine + Celsius + Kelvin + Fahrenheit

Temperature Scales

Factamazoid: Z MACHINE—SURPRISINGLY HOT

They have no idea how they how they did it, but scientists working with the Z machine, the largest X-ray generator in the world, have produced a plasma that is around 130 times hotter than the temperature inside the Sun. The physicists at the Sandia National Laboratories in Albuquerque are openly baffled as to why this plasma is so hot. What is known for sure is that Z—as the scientists simply call it—created a plasma of more than two billion degrees Kelvin, making it hotter than the interior of most stars and, for the time being, the hottest human-made substance in Earth's history. The scientists at Sandia believe that if the causes behind Z's phenomenally hot output were truly understood and harnessed, it would be possible to build smaller, safer nuclear fusion plants capable of producing a greater amount of energy than larger plants.

No. 5, 1948

+

Woman III

+

Boy with a Pipe

+

Portrait of Dr. Gachet

(flip page for answer)

ANSWER

No. 5, 1948 + *Woman III* + *Boy with a Pipe* +
Portrait of Dr. Gachet

Paintings Sold for More Than $100 Million

(by Jackson Pollock, Willem de Kooning, Pablo Picasso,
Vincent Van Gogh)

Factamazoid: WYNN'S LOSS

In 2006, art lovers around the world groaned in disbelief when Steve Wynn, casino magnate and masterpiece collector, put his elbow through Pablo Picasso's 1932 portrait *Le Rêve* (The Dream). Wynn was planning to sell the painting to billionaire collector Steven Cohen for $139 million. The deal was signed, sealed, but not yet delivered, when Wynn, who suffers from an eye disease that affects his peripheral vision, decided to show the painting one last time to some friends. As he showed it, he accidentally gestured too close to the painting and his right elbow went through the canvas.

WHAT'S THE **?** CONNECTION

Paul McCartney

✚

Joan of Arc

✚

Julius Caesar

✚

Luke Perry

(flip page for answer)

ANSWER

Paul McCartney + Joan of Arc + Julius Caesar + Luke Perry

Left-Handed Celebrities

Factamazoid: SOUTHPAW

While using the term *southpaw* to refer to a left-handed person has become commonplace, it was originally used almost exclusively in a sports context. It is generally accepted that the term originated in the United States in the 1840s to refer to left-handed baseball pitchers. Like most outdoor sports, baseball was originally played during the day. Consequently, most ballparks were designed so that the batter faced east, ensuring that the afternoon sun would not shine in his eyes. This meant that left-handed pitchers threw from the south side of the stadium, hence "southpaw." In boxing, someone who boxes left-handed is also referred to as a *southpaw*.

Busecca

➕

Pieds-Paquets à la Marseillaise

➕

Menudo

➕

Haggis

(flip page for answer)

ANSWER

Busecca + Pieds-Paquets à la Marseillaise + Menudo + Haggis

Tripe Dishes

Factamazoid: ROBBIE BURNS NIGHT

The birthday of famous Scottish poet Robert Burns is January 25, and it has become traditional for Scots to gather for a meal on, or near, this date, with haggis as the main dish. Since Scottish vegetarians who know what true haggis is—sheep's stomach (tripe) stuffed with a mixture of oatmeal, lamb's liver, and suet—would probably rather expatriate than eat it, there has been an increasing demand for vegetarian and vegan versions of the dish. A highlight of the meal is the "Address to a Haggis," a mock-heroic poem by Burns that is recited with great gusto, culminating in slashing open the sausage-like haggis bag while intoning the following stanza of Burns's poem:

His knife see rustic Labour dight, / An' cut you up wi' ready sleight, / Trenching your gushing entrails bright, / Like ony ditch; / And then, O what a glorious sight, / Warm-reekin, rich!

WHAT'S THE CONNECTION

German

➕

French

➕

Italian

➕

Romansh

(flip page for answer)

ANSWER

German + French + Italian + Romansh

National Languages of Switzerland

Factamazoid: SWISS WOMEN AND THE VOTE

Amazingly, even though most European women won the right to vote shortly after World War II, the women of Switzerland were not able to vote in federal elections until 1971. The cultural perception of women's role in society being bound to "kinder, kirche, und kuche" (children, church, and kitchen) prompted Switzerland's men to turn down call after call to allow women the federal vote. However, women gradually won the right to vote in various local elections, allowing some women to become prominent politicians. Ironically, in 1968, Geneva had a woman as its mayor—but she still couldn't vote in federal elections. On February 7, 1971, under the pressure of increased international scrutiny, Switzerland finally gave Swiss women federal voting rights.

Now, sir, a war is won!

Put Eliot's toilet up.

Tulsa night life:
filth, gin, a slut.

Go hang a salami,
I'm a lasagna hog.

(flip page for answer)

ANSWER

Now, sir, a war is won! + Put Eliot's toilet up. + Tulsa night life: filth, gin, a slut. + Go hang a salami, I'm a lasagna hog.

Palindromes

(words or phrases that are spelled the same forward and backward.)

Factamazoid Challenge: LIPOGRAMS

Another kind of constrained writing or word game is the lipogram; paragraphs or longer works in which a particular letter or group of letters is missing. What's absent from the following paragraph?

There is something very odd concerning the composition of this body of text. I'm curious, how long will it be before you figure out why this entry is so uncommon?

It looks so modest, you might think nothing is wrong with it! Well, to be truthful, nothing is wrong with it! It is, however, quite distinctive. Study it, scrutinize it very closely, try with the entirety of your intellect to discover the source of this tome's exclusive disposition. If you work tirelessly, without giving up, you might find out!

Answer: The paragraph doesn't contain any "a"s.

THE BIG ! CONNECTION

ambidextrous

+

cauliflower

+

exhaustion

+

mustachioed

+

postneuralgic

+

auctioned

+

tambourine

+

crematorium

+

ulceration

+

sequoia

(flip page for answer)

ANSWER

ambidextrous + cauliflower + exhaustion +
mustachioed + postneuralgic + auctioned +
tambourine + crematorium + ulceration + sequoia

Panvowels

(words that use every vowel once)

AMBIDEXTROUS
CAULIFLOWER
EXHAUSTION
MUSTACHIOED
POSTNEURALGIC
AUCTIONED
TAMBOURINE
CREMATORIUM
ULCERATION
SEQUOIA

WHAT'S THE CONNECTION

Cleopatra

Rosalind

➕

Desdemona

➕

Juliet

(flip page for answer)

ANSWER

Cleopatra + Rosalind + Desdemona + Juliet

Shakespearean Heroines

Factamazoid: WOMEN IN SHAKESPEARE

Though William Shakespeare is often credited as having written some of the finest female roles ever to grace the stage, strictly speaking, he never wrote a single part for a woman. In Shakespeare's time, it was considered highly improper for women to act in plays, so all female parts were played by men or, more often, by feminine young boys. There was never actually any law against women on stage. Apparently, English Renaissance audiences simply considered it unthinkable, as there is no evidence that anyone ever argued in favor of female actors during Shakespeare's lifetime. After the Restoration of the Monarchy in 1660, a more progressive attitude emerged, and actresses began to appear on the English stage, although some parts, such as the nurse in *Romeo and Juliet* and the witches in *Macbeth*, were still played by men for comic effect.

WHAT'S THE CONNECTION

The Jeffersons

+

Maude

+

Good Times

+

Gloria

(flip page for answer)

ANSWER

The Jeffersons + *Maude* + *Good Times* + *Gloria*

All in the Family Spin-Offs

While *All in the Family* spawned several popular spin-offs—*The Jeffersons, Maude, Good Times*—as well as some not-so-popular ones—*Gloria, Archie Bunker's Place*—fans of the show may be surprised to learn of the short-lived 1994 spin-off *704 Hauser Street*. The series is probably one of the weirdest conceptual spin-offs of all time, in that the only connection it has to *All in the Family* is through the house. The old Bunker house was located at *704 Hauser* Street, which, unsurprisingly, was also the setting of the spin-off. Instead of the Bunkers, the show focused on a black couple living in the house. Conceived by Norman Lear as polar opposites to Archie and Edith, Ernie and Rose Cumberbach were a liberal couple with a very conservative son who was married to a Jewish woman. Critical response to *704 Hauser Street* was actually fairly positive, but it was canceled after just five episodes.

Olympus Mons

+

Valles Marineris

+

Hellas Planitia

+

Tharsis Planitia

(flip page for answer)

ANSWER

Olympus Mons + Valles Marineris + Hellas Planitia + Tharsis Planitia

Geological Features of the Planet Mars

Factamazoid: OLYMPUS MONS

At a height of more than 16 miles (26 km), Mars's massive volcano, Olympus Mons, is the highest point in the solar system. Nearly three times taller than Mt. Everest, the volcano is also more than 360 miles (600 km) across. Mons is so massive that a person standing on the surface of Mars would be unable to view the top of the volcano even from a great distance, because the curvature of the planet and the volcano itself would obscure it. With a peak that reaches above most of the Martian atmosphere, scientists calculate that Olympus Mons could not exist on Earth. Due to Earth's stronger gravity field, the massive volcano would collapse under its own weight.

WHAT'S THE ? CONNECTION

Pinatubo

Etna

Pelée

Kilauea

(flip page for answer)

ANSWER

Pinatubo + Etna + Pelée + Kilauea

Active Volcanoes

Factamazoid: MAUNA LOA, BIGGEST MOUNTAIN ON EARTH

While Mt. Everest holds the title for the highest elevation on land, the active Hawaiian volcano Mauna Loa is actually the biggest mountain on the planet. The misconception stems from the fact that only some 13,448 feet (4100 m) of Mauna Loa are above sea level, making it appear to be a fairly average mountain. However, when measured from its true base at the bottom of the ocean, Mauna Loa's total height exceeds that of Everest by more than three fourths of a mile (1.2 km). If you want to get really technical, Mauna Loa's neighbor, Mauna Kea, is actually the tallest mountain in the world—about 350 feet (107 meters) taller than Mauna Loa—but Mauna Kea's mass by volume doesn't compare to that of Mauna Loa, which is estimated at approximately 18,000 cubic miles (75,000 square km), making Mauna Loa the biggest mountain on Earth.

WHAT'S THE CONNECTION

Socrates

+

Cleopatra

+

Juan Ponce de Léon

+

Grigori Rasputin

(flip page for answer)

ANSWER

Socrates + Cleopatra + Juan Ponce de Léon + Grigori Rasputin

Poisoned

(Socrates was murdered by drinking hemlock; Cleopatra committed suicide by an asp's bite; Ponce de Léon was fatally shot by a poisoned arrow; Rasputin survived being fed cyanide-laced cakes and wine.)

Factamazoid: THE DEATH OF RASPUTIN

Russian mystic Grigori Rasputin's murder is the stuff of legend. On December 16, 1916, a group of noble-men lured Rasputin to Prince Felix Yusupov's Moika Palace, where they fed him cakes and red wine laced with cyanide. Amazingly, Rasputin was unaffected. Next, Yusupov shot Rasputin in the back, but when he leaned over to check the body, Rasputin opened his eyes, attacked him, and ran outside. The pursuing nobles shot Rasputin three more times before they finally clubbed him into submission, wrapped him in a sheet, and threw him into the freezing Neva River. Three days later, when his body was found, the cause of death was determined to be hypothermia.

WHAT'S THE CONNECTION

El Cordobés

Paquiro

Juan Belmonte

El Viti

(flip page for answer)

ANSWER

El Cordobés + Paquiro + Juan Belmonte + El Viti

Spanish Bullfighters

Factamazoid: THE RUNNING OF THE NUDES

Each year, thousands of naked protesters, many wearing only plastic horns and red scarves, race through Pamplona's winding streets to promote a humane alternative to the Running of the Bulls. Supported by animal welfare groups, including PETA, the Running of the Nudes occurs two days before the Running of the Bulls, just before the start of the nine-day festival of San Fermín. The Nudes follow the same route as the Bulls, from the Santo Domingo corrals through the town's streets, ending at the Plaza de Toros. Local citizens, initially offended by the public display of nudity, have become more accepting recently because, ironically, the Nudes have actually made the festival more popular, drawing more spectators than ever and increasing the event's economic impact on the town.

WHAT'S THE CONNECTION

Blanco

+

Reposado

+

Añejo

+

Joven Abocado

(flip page for answer)

ANSWER

Blanco + Reposado + Añejo + Joven Abocado

Grades of Tequila

Factamazoid: TEQUILA

As tequila's popularity has increased around the world, the Mexican government has vigorously fought to protect the name of its cherished spirit. In international agreements, including the North American Free Trade Agreement (NAFTA), tequila is protected as a "geographically indicated product" under intellectual property rights law. In 1997, an agreement was reached between Mexico and Europe giving tequila a denomination of origin classification, making Mexico the only place in the world where an agave spirit can lawfully be labeled *tequila*. Furthermore, the spirit must be fermented from the blue agave plant indigenous to the state of Jalisco, Mexico, and nearby areas. If not produced according to these restrictions, it is called *mezcal*. Other denomination-of-origin alcoholic beverages include scotch, sherry, cognac, and champagne.

THE BIG ! CONNECTION

Call a pig Napoleon.

➕

Walk around the house naked.

➕

Walk on the right-hand side of a footpath.

➕

Wear a skirt (males).

➕

Hunt for whales.

➕

Possess cow while intoxicated.

➕

Urinate while standing up (males after 10 P.M.).

➕

Wear a red hat and walk down Het Meyer (main street).

➕

Bring bears to the beach.

➕

Spay a female dog or cat.

(flip page for answer)

ANSWER

Call a pig Napoleon. ✦ Walk around the house naked. ✦ Walk on the right-hand side of a footpath. ✦ Wear a skirt (males). ✦ Hunt for whales. ✦ Possess cow while intoxicated. ✦ Urinate while standing up (males after 10 P.M.). ✦ Wear a red hat and walk down Het Meyer (main street). ✦ Bring bears to the beach. ✦ Spay a female dog or cat.

Against the Law

CALL A PIG NAPOLEON: **Illegal in France**

WALK AROUND THE HOUSE NAKED: **Illegal in Singapore**

WALK ON THE RIGHT-HAND SIDE OF A FOOTPATH: **Illegal in Australia**

WEAR A SKIRT (MALES): **Illegal in Italy**

HUNT FOR WHALES: **Illegal in Oklahoma**

POSSESS COW WHILE INTOXICATED: **Illegal in Scotland**

URINATE WHILE STANDING UP (MALES AFTER 10 P.M.):

Illegal in Switzerland

WEAR A RED HAT AND WALK DOWN HET MEYER (MAIN STREET):

Illegal in Antwerp, Belgium

BRING BEARS TO THE BEACH: **Illegal in Israel**

SPAY A FEMALE DOG OR CAT: **Illegal in Norway**

WHAT'S THE CONNECTION

Cuttlefish

Geoduck

+

Garden Snail

+

Pink Mucket

(flip page for answer)

107

ANSWER

Cuttlefish + Geoduck + Garden Snail + Pink Mucket

Mollusks

Factamazoid: CUTTLEFISH CAMOUFLAGE

When it comes to camouflage, cuttlefish are able to change their appearance with a speed and diversity unmatched in the animal kingdom. Relatives of the octopus and squid, cuttlefish are actually mollusks, and can be found in coastal waters around the world. With little else to protect it, the cuttlefish's camouflage wizardry is essential to its survival. As it senses different patterns, its large brain triggers pigments, and reflective cells in its skin transform into almost any color or pattern. In addition, tiny muscles give the cuttlefish's skin the ability to transform its texture. A cuttlefish will often display one pattern or texture with half of its body while the other half takes on another. Amazingly, scientists have determined that cuttlefish are actually color blind, relying on sensing contrast rather than color to make their amazing patterns.

WHAT'S THE CONNECTION

Cistercians (Chimay)

➕

Dominicans (Maraschino)

➕

Carthusians (Chartreuse)

➕

Benedictines (Benedictine)

(flip page for answer)

ANSWER

Cistercians (Chimay) + Dominicans (Maraschino) + Carthusians (Chartreuse) + Benedictines (Benedictine)

Monastic Orders and their Alcoholic Beverages

Factamazoid: CHARTREUSE COCKTAIL RECIPES

CHARTREUSE EXPERIENCE

1 part Green Chartreuse

1 part vodka

5 parts orange juice

1 part lemon juice

Combine over ice in a highball glass.

THE SCREAMING LIZARD

2 parts Green Chartreuse

1 part tequila

Layer ingredients in a shot glass with Chartreuse on the bottom. Can be served flaming.

CHARTINI

1 part Green Chartreuse

3 parts gin

Shake ingredients in a cocktail shaker with ice. Strain into a cocktail glass.

WHAT'S THE ? CONNECTION

Lester Horwitz

+

Harry Moses Horwitz

+

Samuel Horwitz

+

Louis Feinberg

(flip page for answer)

ANSWER

Lester Horwitz + Harry Moses Horwitz + Samuel Horwitz + Louis Feinberg

Three Stooges

Factamazoid: THREE STOOGES

The Three Stooges started in 1925 as part of a bawdy vaudeville act called Ted Healy and His Stooges. In the act, Healy would attempt to sing or tell jokes while his incompetent assistants, brothers Moe and Shemp Howard and violinist-comedian Larry Fine, would keep "interrumping" him. After a decade of tense partnership with Healy, the Stooges broke out on their own in 1934. Both revered and reviled for their broad and violent brand of slapstick, the Three Stooges polarized critics and audiences. The following observation, from a 1937 issue of *Motion Picture Herald*, remains as true today as when it was written: "The public appears ... to be divided roughly into two groups, one composed of persons who laugh at the Three Stooges and the other made up of those who wonder why."

WHAT'S THE CONNECTION

Second Punic
(218–202 B.C.)

+

Saxon
(772–804 A.D.)

+

Mexican-American
(1846–1848 A.D.)

+

Anglo-Zanzibar
(August 27, 1896)

(flip page for answer)

ANSWER

Second Punic + **Saxon** + **Mexican-American** + **Anglo-Zanzibar**

Wars

Factamazoid: SHORTEST WAR

Lasting just 38 minutes, the Anglo-Zanzibar War holds the record for the shortest war in recorded history. The conflict was precipitated by the death of Zanzibar's British-friendly sultan Hamad bin Thuwaini. The British quickly tried to install their chosen replacement, but the dead Sultan's brother-in-law, Sayyid Khalid bin Barghash seized control. The British responded by stationing five warships in the harbor in front of the palace and issuing an ultimatum for Barghash to abdicate by 9:00 A.M. on the 27th. The deadline passed, and at 9:02 A.M. the British opened fire. Zanzibar's only ship—Barghash's yacht, *The Glasglow*—was hit and sunk at 9:15, and by 9:40 Barghash had surrendered and fled to German East Africa.

WHAT'S THE ? CONNECTION

Lord of Mann

Knight of the Elephant

➕

The White Heron

➕

Paramount Chief of Fiji

(flip page for answer)

ANSWER

**Lord of Mann + Knight of the Elephant +
The White Heron + Paramount Chief of Fiji**

Titles Held by
Queen Elizabeth II of England

Factamazoid: QUEEN ELIZABETH II IN UNIFORM

Queen Elizabeth II is the first, and so far only, female member of the British royal family to actually serve in the armed forces. When World War II broke out, it was suggested that thirteen-year-old Elizabeth and her younger sister, Princess Margaret, should be sent to Canada. Their mother famously refused to consider this, saying, "The children could not possibly go without me, I wouldn't leave without the King, and the King won't leave under any circumstances." In 1945, the nineteen-year-old Elizabeth convinced her father to let her join the Women's Auxiliary Territorial Service, where she trained as a driver.

THE BIG ! CONNECTION

Rookery
+
Pace
+
Quiver
+
Business
+
Smack
+
Murder
+
Tower
+
Mischief
+
Crash
+
Escargatoire

(flip page for answer)

ANSWER

Rookery + Pace + Quiver + Business + Smack + Murder + Tower + Mischief + Crash + Escargatoire

Animal Groupings

ROOKERY: **Albatross**

PACE: **Donkeys, asses**

QUIVER: **Cobras**

BUSINESS: **Ferrets, flies**

SMACK: **Jellyfish**

MURDER: **Crows, magpies**

TOWER: **Giraffes**

MISCHIEF: **Mice**

CRASH: **Rhinoceroses (also called a stubbornness)**

ESCARGATOIRE: **Snails**

The Flash

➕

Apache Chief

➕

Black Vulcan

➕

Gleek

(flip page for answer)

ANSWER

The Flash + Apache Chief + Black Vulcan + Gleek

Super Friends Members

WHAT'S THE ? CONNECTION

Franz Schubert

➕

Al Capone

➕

Vladimir Lenin

➕

Howard Hughes

(flip page for answer)

ANSWER

Franz Schubert + Al Capone + Vladimir Lenin + Howard Hughes

Died from Syphilis

Factamazoid: SYPHILIS, THE (INSERT COUNTRY) DISEASE

The country of origin of venereal syphilis has been debated since the disease ravaged Europe in the late fifteenth and the early sixteenth centuries. Author Desiderius Erasmus considered nothing more horrible than the French Disease, or syphilis. In his *Colloquies*, he writes: "In a showdown, it wouldn't yield to leprosy, elephantisis, ringworm, gout, or sycosis." Understandably, the French objected to this, calling it the Italian Disease. So began the trend of each country using it to insult a rival country. The Russians called it the Polish Disease, impugning their neighbors to the west, who predictably called it the Russian Disease. It was called the British Disease by Tahitians, while the Turks, leaving nationality out of the matter altogether, simply called it the Christian Disease.

WHAT'S THE CONNECTION?

Faber-Castell

Bentcil

Grifos

Pentel

(flip page for answer)

ANSWER

Faber-Castell + Bentcil + Grifos + Pentel

Pencil Manufacturers

Factamazoid: UNLEADED PENCILS

Despite their name, "lead" pencils have always been made of graphite, never lead. The confusion began in the mid-sixteenth century, when an enormous deposit of a black substance was found in Borrowdale, England. The Englishmen who discovered it believed it to be lead, so they called it *plumbago* (lead ore). The locals soon began using the material to mark their sheep, and before long, someone found that plumbago made excellent marks on paper. Plumbago could be sawed into a stick, wrapped in a bit of sheepskin, and carried around. Eventually the sheepskin was replaced by wood. In 1779, English scientist K.W. Scheele discovered that the substance was not actually lead, but a type of carbon instead. In 1789, German geologist Abraham Gottlob Werner named it *graphite*, after the Greek word meaning "to write."

WHAT'S THE CONNECTION

Affenpinscher

Malamute

Schipperke

Puli

(flip page for answer)

ANSWER

Affenpinscher + Malamute + Schipperke + Puli

Dog Breeds

Factamazoid: RATTING

In the 1800s, the sport of rat baiting, or "ratting," was enormously popular among North American and British working classes. In backroom "rat pits," enthusiasts would wager as to which dog could kill the most rats in a given time. Ratters, as the dogs were called, were typically small with powerful jaws—often terrier breeds, including the bull terrier, fox terrier, Jack Russell terrier, rat terrier, Staffordshire bull terrier, and affenpinscher. Eventually, public distaste for the inhumane sport forced its decline, and by the end of the nineteenth century, rat baiting had faded into near obscurity. Because of their feisty temperaments and playful natures, many of the ratter breeds became popular house pets—including the clownish affenpinscher, which has been bred in Germany since the seventeenth century. It's no coincidence that the name *Affenpinscher* roughly translates to English as "monkey terrier."

THE BIG ! CONNECTION

1933 Double Eagle

Sumatran striped rabbit

Bombay Phenotype (HH)

Cornish

Rafflesia

Wollemi Pine

Francium

Ethiopian wolf

Osmium

Bingham's Syndrome

(flip page for answer)

1933 Double Eagle + Sumatran striped rabbit + Bombay Phenotype (HH) + Cornish + Rafflesia + Wollemi Pine + Francium + Ethiopian wolf + Osmium + Bingham's Syndrome

World's Rarest

1933 DOUBLE EAGLE: coin

SUMATRAN STRIPED RABBIT: rabbit

BOMBAY PHENOTYPE (HH): blood type

CORNISH: language

RAFFLESIA: flower

WOLLEMI PINE: tree

FRANCIUM: element

ETHIOPIAN WOLF: dog

OSMIUM: metal

BINGHAM'S SYNDROME: disease

Ruy Lopez

+

Giuco Piano

+

King's Gambit

+

Bogo-Indian

(flip page for answer)

ANSWER

Ruy Lopez + Giuco Piano + King's Gambit + Bogo-Indian

Chess Moves

Factamazoid: "THE TURK"

"The Turk" was the Deep Blue of the late eighteenth century, a turban-wearing, chess-playing automaton that defeated all comers. At the time, automatons were the hottest fad: the public flocked to see mechanical ducks, elephants, and human mannequins that could write, draw, and play musical instruments. Designed and constructed in 1770 by Austrian-Hungarian baron Wolfgang von Kempelen, the Turk appeared to actually play chess, executing complex strategies and outplaying some of Europe's finest chess players. It was, of course, a hoax—a chessmaster operated the Turk from a cleverly hidden compartment within the cabinet that allegedly housed its gears. Charles Babbage, the godfather of the computer, played two games against the Turk, and contemporary scientists frequently credit the machine for provoking questions about what we now call "artificial intelligence."

Béchamel

+

Mole

+

Hoisin

+

Garum

(flip page for answer)

ANSWER

Béchamel + Mole + Hoisin + Garum

Sauces

Factamazoid: GARUM

One of the most popular condiments of its day, garum, a pickled fish sauce, was a mainstay in ancient Roman society. Taking its name from *garus*, the fish originally used in its production, garum appears in most of the recipes featured in the famous Roman cookbook *Apicius*. The sauce was generally made by crushing the innards of various fish, such as tuna, eel, and others, and fermenting them in brine. While the sauce was famously mild and subtle in flavor, the actual production of garum created such awful smells that garum factories were usually banished to the outskirts of cities. Contrary to present-day preference, the main objective of ancient sauces seemed to be to disguise the natural taste of food, possibly to conceal questionable freshness. This theory is supported by a sauce recipe in *Apicius*, which concludes with the author's boast, "At table, no one will know what he is eating."

Brainy

+

Hefty

+

Vanity

+

Clockwork

(flip page for answer)

ANSWER

Brainy + Hefty + Vanity + Clockwork

Smurfs

Factamazoid: HOYT CURTIN

Hoyt Curtin is frequently recognized as the king of the commercial jingle, having penned some of pop culture's most hummable tunes. In 1957, while Curtin was working on a jingle for Schlitz beer, a chance meeting with budding cartoon producers William Hanna and Joseph Barbera sparked one of the most fruitful collaborations in cartoon history.

Eventually, Curtin wrote the tunes for more than 250 Hanna Barbera shows, including *The Flintstones*; *The Jetsons*; *Tom and Jerry*; *The Yogi Bear Show*; *Top Cat*; *The Magilla Gorilla Show*; *Josie and the Pussycats*; *Scooby-Doo, Where Are You!*; *Quick Draw McGraw*; *The Huckleberry Hound Show*; *Jonny Quest*; and, his final project for Hanna-Barbera, *The Smurfs*.

Post

+

Homogenic

+

Telegram

+

Vespertine

(flip page for answer)

ANSWER

Post + **Homogenic** + *Telegram* + *Vespertine*

Björk Albums

Factamazoid: ICELANDIC NAMES

Most Icelanders do not have a family name, such as Smith, Jones, or Sajak. Instead, Icelandic "last names" are formed by taking the name of a child's father and adding either "son" or "dottir." Let's say Thor has a son named Jon and a daughter named Frida. The son's name would be Jon Thorson while the daughter's would be Frida Thorsdottir. Because they don't have surnames, it is not appropriate to call an Icelander by "Mr." or "Ms." This means that Icelanders are on a first-name basis with everyone—including their president. In the telephone directory, Icelanders are listed alphabetically by first name. Although famous Icelander Björk is commonly teased for taking what some perceive to be a pretentious stage name, Björk Guðmundsdóttir simply goes by her first name, as any Icelander would address her, whether formally or casually.

WHAT'S THE CONNECTION

Miltonduff

Dimple

➕

Inchgower

➕

Glenlochy

(flip page for answer)

ANSWER

Miltonduff + Dimple + Inchgower + Glenlochy

Brands of Whiskey

Factamazoid: DRUNK ANTS

In his 1882 book *Ants, Bees, and Wasps*, naturalist Sir John Lubbock wrote the following after studying intoxicated ants:

"It has been suggested that the ants of each nest have some sign or password by which they recognize one another... I decided therefore to intoxicate them. I took fifty specimens, twenty-five from one nest and twenty-five from another, made them dead drunk, marked each with a spot of paint, and put them on a table close to where the other ants from one of the nests were feeding... The ants which were feeding soon noticed those which I had made drunk... The strangers they took to the edge of the moat and dropped into the water, while they bore their friends home into the nest, where by degrees they slept off the effects of the spirit. Thus it is evident that they know their friends even when incapable of giving any sign or password."

WHAT'S THE ? CONNECTION

Joey

➕

Ritchie

➕

Johnny

➕

Dee Dee

(flip page for answer)

ANSWER

Joey + Richie + Johnny + Dee Dee

Ramones

Factamazoid: RAMONES VS. SPECTOR

In a now famous session in 1980, pioneering punks The Ramones brought in legendary producer Phil Spector to polish their sound. The album they produced together, *End of the Century*, contains some of the Ramones's most famous songs. The sessions also spawned another of Spector's infamous gun incidents. As the story goes, Spector forced the band to play the opening guitar chord to "Rock and Roll High School" for eight solid hours. When the frustrated Ramones attempted to leave, Spector pulled a gun on the group and forced them to play his 1963 song "Baby I Love You." The story was later confirmed by Joey Ramone: "That's true, it was insane, he locked us in his house for hours, and he pulled a gun on Dee Dee. But it was a positive learning experience. And that chord does sound really good."

WHAT'S THE CONNECTION

Phobos

➕

Io

➕

Hyperion

➕

Luna

(flip page for answer)

ANSWER

Phobos + Io + Hyperion + Luna

Moons

Factamazoid: PLANETS AND THEIR MOONS

Saturn has 33 moons, while Jupiter boasts 62 of them—24 unnamed. Here is a list of the other known moons in our solar system:

EARTH	1	Moon (Luna)
PLUTO	1	Charon
MARS	2	Phobos, Deimos
NEPTUNE	13	Triton, Nereid, Naiad, Thalassa, Despina, Galatea, Larissa, Proteus, plus 5 unnamed
URANUS	27	Cordelia, Ophelia, Bianca, Cressida, Desdemona, Juliet, Portia, Rosalind, Belinda, Puck, Miranda, Ariel, Umbriel, Titania, Oberon, Caliban, Sycorax, Prospero, Setebos, Stephano, Trinculo, plus 6 unnamed

WHAT'S THE ? CONNECTION

Kelly

+

Carrie

+

Bring Back Birdie

+

Moose Murders

(flip page for answer)

ANSWER

Kelly + Carrie + Bring Back Birdie + Moose Murders

Broadway Flops

Factamazoid: *CARRIE, THE MUSICAL*

Generally considered to be the biggest flop in Broadway history, the 1988 musical *Carrie* closed less than 72 hours after it opened. Adapted from Stephen King's 1974 best-selling novel about a tormented teenager with psychic powers, the musical was originally produced by the Royal Shakespeare Company in London, where it received mixed reviews. Despite this lukewarm reception, the producers transferred the show to Broadway at an expense of more than $8 million. After 15 previews, plagued by script and technical problems—such as Carrie's body microphone shorting out whenever the fake blood was poured on her—the production opened on May 12, 1988, at the Virginia Theater. The critics were brutal, and the show closed after only five performances, losing more than $7 million and securing its place in theater history as one of the most expensive disasters of all time.

Erich Hartmann

+

Hiroyoshi Nishizawa

+

Marmaduke Pattle

+

Pappy Boyington

(flip page for answer)

ANSWER

Erich Hartmann + Hiroyoshi Nishizawa +
Marmaduke Pattle + Pappy Boyington

WWII Fighter-Pilot Aces

Factamazoid: SOME FIGHTER-PILOT ACES OF WWII

COUNTRY	NAME OF PILOT	VICTORIES
Germany	Erich Hartmann	352
Finland	Eino Juutilainen	94
Japan	Hiroyoshi Nishizawa	87
Soviet Union	Ivan Kozhedub	62
Romania	Prince Constantine Cantacuzene	60
South Africa	Marmaduke Pattle	51
Croatia	Mato Dukovac	40
United States	Richard Bong	40
Great Britain	James Johnson	38
Hungary	Dezsõ Szentgyorgyi	34
France	Pierre Closterman	33
Czechoslovakia	Jan Režòak	32

THE BIG ● CONNECTION

Jean/Marie
➕
Jean/Marie
➕
Jean/Marie
➕
Jean/Marie
➕
Jean/Marie
➕
Phillippe/Catherine
➕
Christophe/Nathalie
➕
Nicolas/Celine
➕
Kevin/Elodie
➕
Thomas/Lea

(flip page for answer)

ANSWER

Jean/Marie + Jean/Marie + Jean/Marie + Jean/Marie +
Jean/Marie + Phillippe/Catherine + Christophe/Nathalie +
Nicolas/Celine + Kevin/Elodie + Thomas/Lea

Most Popular Boy/Girl Names
in France (by Year)

JEAN/MARIE: 1910
JEAN/MARIE: 1920
JEAN/MARIE: 1930
JEAN/MARIE: 1940
JEAN/MARIE: 1950
PHILLIPPE/CATHERINE: 1960
CHRISTOPHE/NATHALIE: 1970
NICOLAS/CELINE: 1980
KEVIN/ELODIE: 1990
THOMAS/LEA: 2000

According to MeilleursPrenoms.com

WHAT'S THE ? CONNECTION

Jimmy Dorsey

+

Woody Herman

+

Artie Shaw

+

Pee Wee Russell

(flip page for answer)

ANSWER

Jimmy Dorsey + Woody Herman + Artie Shaw + Pee Wee Russell

Jazz Clarinetists

Factamazoid: WOODY ALLEN, JAZZ CLARINETIST

Celebrated film director Woody Allen is a passionate fan of jazz clarinet and an accomplished clarinetist in his own right. Allen, who chose his stage name from his idol, famed clarinetist Woody Herman, has played the clarinet since adolescence and has recorded and performed publicly since the late 1960s, notably with the Preservation Hall Jazz Band on the soundtrack of his film *Sleeper*.

Despite having been nominated for 21 Academy Awards and winning three, Allen has consistently refused to attend the ceremony or acknowledge his Oscar wins, as he believes bestowing awards on works of art is a meaningless exercise. Allen has famously stated that he is unable to attend the Oscars because his New Orleans Jazz Band plays every Monday evening at Manhattan's Carlyle Hotel.

I Do, I Do, I Do, I Do, I Do

Love Isn't Easy
(But It Sure Is Hard Enough)

Put On Your White Sombrero

The Winner Takes It All

(flip page for answer)

ANSWER

I Do, I Do, I Do, I Do, I Do ✦ Love Isn't Easy (But It Sure Is Hard Enough) ✦ Put On Your White Sombrero ✦ The Winner Takes It All

ABBA Songs

Factamazoid: BJÖRN AGAIN

Taking their name from ABBA founder Björn Ulvaeus, Björn Again is an enormously popular franchise of touring ABBA tribute bands. Created in 1988 by Australians Rod Leissle and John Tyrrell, there are currently five Björn Agains performing all over the world. Björn Again takes a very lighthearted approach to their portrayal of ABBA but remains faithful to the songs themselves. Björn Again members talk to the audience in a faux-Swedish accent, and take stage names that poke fun at the original group's names: Agnetha Falstart, Benny Anderwear, Frida Longstokin, and Björn Volvo-us. In the words of ABBA's Benny Andersson: "Fans had better make the most of Björn Again because that's the closest they are going to get to seeing ABBA!"

French Lop

+

Dwarf Hotot

+

Flemish Giant

+

English Spot

(flip page for answer)

ANSWER

French Lop + Dwarf Hotot + Flemish Giant + English Spot

Rabbit Breeds

Factamazoid: THE AUSTRALIAN RABBIT WAR

Australia's rabbit problems began in 1859, when Aussie landowner Thomas Austin arranged for 24 wild rabbits to be shipped from England so that he could release them on his property and hunt them for sport. Austin and his friends had so much fun that soon, more rabbits were released on estates across the Australian countryside. Incredibly, by 1900 an infestation of more than 300 million rabbits covered the entire Australian continent. Nearly one-eighth of Australia's native mammal species were wiped out. Plants went extinct, and soil was ruined. After ineffective attempts to corral the rabbits with "rabbit-proof fences," the Australian government resorted to chemical warfare in the 1950s. After the spreading of myxoma, an experimental virus, the rabbit population dropped from its peak of 600 million to 100 million.

WHAT'S THE ? CONNECTION

Smarty Jones

+

Spend a Buck

+

Donerail

+

Sea Hero

(flip page for answer)

ANSWER

Smarty Jones + Spend a Buck + Donerail + Sea Hero

Kentucky Derby Winners

Factamazoid: DONERAIL

First run in 1875, the Kentucky Derby is the longest-running continuously held sporting event in the United States. Over the years, the race has seen its share of upsets, but the greatest upset of all came in 1913 when a 91-1 longshot named Donerail won the 39th Kentucky Derby. Going into the race, the only thing most people knew about Donerail was that he was an undistinguished three-year-old bay colt bred and trained in Kentucky by T.P. Hayes. At the start of the race, Donerail showed restrained speed, keeping pace with the other horses, but going into the final turn, Donerail and jockey Roscoe Goose made their move with a sudden burst of speed. Donerail drew away from the field in the final 16th of the race, setting a new track record in the process. Those fortunate few who picked Donerail to win enjoyed a $184.90 payoff for a $2 bet.

WHAT'S THE ? CONNECTION

Young Chang

+

Weber

+

Baldwin

+

Bösendorfer

(flip page for answer)

157

ANSWER

Young Chang + **Weber** + **Baldwin** + **Bösendorfer**

Piano Manufacturers

Factamazoid: THE CELEBRATED CHOP WALTZ

Although you might include it in a list of reasons to keep a piano keyboard locked, the "Celebrated Chop Waltz," or "Chopsticks," as it is more commonly known, is one of the most famous and most-performed pieces of piano music in the world. Some of the world's greatest composers, including Alexander Borodin and Nikolai Rimsky-Korsakov, have been inspired to write variations on the piece, originally written in 1877 by a 16-year-old British girl named Euphemia Allen. Perhaps in an effort to be taken more seriously, it was published under the pseudonym Arthur de Lulli. The song title is explained by the instructions on the original piece, which read: "play with both hands turned sideways, the little fingers lowest, so that the movements of the hands imitate the chopping from which this waltz gets its name."

Shem

➕

Japheth

➕

Ham

➕

His Wife

(flip page for answer)

ANSWER

Shem + Japheth + Ham + His Wife

Noah's Family

Factamazoid: NOAH'S NAMELESS WIFE

Noah's wife, one of eight people handpicked by God to survive the flood, preserve Earth's animal life, and repopulate the planet, is arguably one of the most important characters in the Bible. However, she is never specifically mentioned by name. Though the story of the Flood and Noah's Ark, found in Genesis chapters six to nine, frequently mentions Noah and his three sons, Shem, Ham, and Japheth, by name, the same does not apply to their wives. Noah's wife is referenced a total of five times in Genesis, but she is spoken about as only one in a group. While some ancient Jewish traditions say that Noah married his niece, Amzarach, daughter of Rachel, the most widely held belief is that Noah's wife was Naamah, the sister of Tubal-Cain.

Tony Esposito

+

Oliver Levi Seibert

+

Grant Fuhr

+

Vladislav Tretiak

(flip page for answer)

ANSWER

Tony Esposito + Oliver Levi Seibert + Grant Fuhr + Vladislav Tretiak

Hockey Hall of Fame Goalies

Between 1993 and 1999, Attila Ambrus, sometimes called the worst goalie in the history of professional hockey, robbed 29 banks, post offices, and travel agencies in Hungary. As a member of UTE, a professional Hungarian hockey team, Ambrus once gave up 23 goals in a game and 88 in a memorable five-game stretch. Desperate for cash, he turned to crime, becoming a national hero in the process. Wearing a hodge-podge of bad costumes and wigs, he gave flowers to female bank tellers during robberies and mailed bottles of wine to the investigators trying to catch him. The media dubbed him the Whiskey Robber because witnesses claimed they saw him down shots of Johnnie Walker in a bar across from a bank before robbing it. He was caught in 1999 and sentenced to 17 years in prison.

WHAT'S THE ? CONNECTION

Britva

Tolchock

Horrorshow

Droog

(flip page for answer)

ANSWER

Britva + Tolchock + Horrorshow + Droog

Nadsat

(slang from *A Clockwork Orange*)

Factamazoid: NADSAT

Nadsat is a Russian-influenced form of English slang, ingeniously invented by author Anthony Burgess for Alex, the anti-hero and narrator of his controversial novel *A Clockwork Orange*. Burgess, who was fluent in several languages, developed Nadsat, which gets its name from the Russian word for "teen," because he wanted Alex to have a unique voice, and he feared that using contemporary slang would date the book. Burgess did not approve of the inclusion of a glossary in one edition, because he wanted to force readers to "learn" Nadsat as they read. Some key vocabulary:

horrorshow: good, well
britva: knife, razor
Charlie: chaplain/priest

gulliver: head
bezoomy: mad
cancer: cigarette

bolshy: big
droog: friend
tolchock: hit

WHAT'S THE CONNECTION

Pierre Bezukhov

+

Andrew Bolkonski

+

Natasha Rostova

+

General Kutuzov

(flip page for answer)

ANSWER

Pierre Bezukhov + Andrew Bolkonski + Natasha Rostova + General Kutuzov

War and Peace Characters

Factamazoid: WAR AND THE WORLD?

Seinfeld fans, of course, remember the episode in which Jerry tells Elaine that the original title of Tolstoy's *War and Peace* was *War, What Is It Good For?* Although history doesn't quite support this account, there has actually been some debate regarding the title. The confusion stems from the fact that the Russian words for *peace* and *world*, which were traditionally homophones in Russian with different spellings, took on identical spellings after the Bolshevik reforms of 1918. This led to a theory in the Soviet Union that the original manuscript was called *War and the World* or *War and Society*. However, considering that Tolstoy himself translated the title into French as *La Guerre et la Paix* (*War and Peace*), the prevailing opinion is that *War and Peace* is the correct title.

WHAT'S THE CONNECTION

Ramón Mercader

Byron De La Beckwith

Brutus

Jacques Clément

(flip page for answer)

ANSWER

Ramón Mercader + **Byron De La Beckwith** + **Brutus** + **Jacques Clément**

Assassins

Factamazoid: ASSASSIN MATCH

Match the assassin with his or her victim:

1. Charles J. Guiteau
2. Jack Ruby
3. Yigal Amir
4. Byron De La Beckwith
5. Marcus Junius Brutus
6. Charlotte Corday
7. Ramón Mercader
8. Nathuram Godse

a. Medgar Evers
b. James Garfield
c. Mahatma Gandhi
d. Jean-Paul Marat
e. Yitzhak Rabin
f. Lee Harvey Oswald
g. Leon Trotsky
h. Julius Caesar

Answers 1. b; 2. f; 3. e; 4. a; 5. h; 6. d; 7. g; 8. c

Pageboy

+

Tonsure

+

Mullet

+

Mohawk

(flip page for answer)

ANSWER

Pageboy + **Tonsure** + **Mullet** + **Mohawk**

Hairstyles

Factamazoid: CLONY MAN, IRON-AGE PUNKER

For centuries, the Mohawk hairstyle was attributed to the Huron Native Americans of the Great Lakes region. However, in the Irish town of Clonycavan in 2003, a peat harvester made a discovery that would change hair history forever—a 2,300-year-old corpse, remarkably well-preserved by the unique chemistry of a peat bog, looking ready to rock, crowned with an unmistakable "hawk."

What's more, Clonycavan Man, "Clony" for short, had imported hair product in his hair—a gel made from vegetable oil mixed with a resin from southwestern France or Spain. This may attest to trade between Ireland and southern Europe. The gel also leads some scientists to speculate that Clonycavan Man was wealthy, as only an affluent guy could afford imported cosmetics.

THE BIG ! CONNECTION

Helium

+

Pronghorn

+

Africa

+

John Adams

+

Linus

+

Tenzing Norgay

+

Eastern Brown Snake

+

Islam

+

Edwin Eugene Aldrin, Jr.

+

Sandy Allen

(flip page for answer)

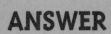

ANSWER

Helium + **Pronghorn** + **Africa** + **John Adams** + **Linus** +
Tenzing Norgay + **Eastern Brown Snake** +
Islam + **Edwin Eugene Aldrin, Jr.** + **Sandy Allen**

They are all seconds.

HELIUM: **second-lightest element**

PRONGHORN: **second-fastest land animal**

AFRICA: **second-largest continent**

JOHN ADAMS: **second President**

LINUS: **second Pope**

TENZING NORGAY: **second to set foot on the summit of Everest**

EASTERN BROWN SNAKE: **second-most-venomous snake in the world**

ISLAM: **second-most-popular religion in the world**

EDWIN EUGENE ALDRIN, JR.: **(a.k.a. Buzz Aldrin)**
second man to walk on the moon

SANDY ALLEN: **second-tallest woman in the world**

INDEX